LAY OUT THE LUNGS

By Kirsty Holmes

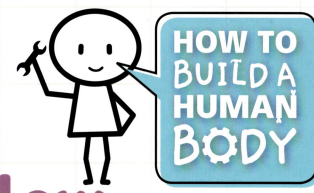

HOW TO BUILD A HUMAN BODY

Enslow PUBLISHING

Published in 2021 by Enslow Publishing, LLC
101 W. 23rd Street, Suite 240,
New York, NY 10011

Copyright © 2021 Booklife Publishing
This edition is published by arrangement with Booklife Publishing

All rights reserved.

No part of this book may be reproduced by any means without the written permission of the publisher.

Cataloging-in-Publication Data

Names: Holmes, Kirsty.
Title: Lay out the lungs / Kirsty Holmes.
Description: New York : Enslow Publishing, 2021. | Series: How to build a human body | Includes glossary and index.
Identifiers: ISBN 9781978519190 (pbk.) | ISBN 9781978519213 (library bound) | ISBN 9781978519206 (6 pack)
Subjects: LCSH: Lungs--Juvenile literature. | Respiratory organs--Juvenile literature. | Human physiology--Juvenile literature.
Classification: LCC QP121.H65 2020 | DDC 612.2'4--dc23

Printed in the United States of America

CPSIA compliance information: Batch #BS20ENS: For further information contact Enslow Publishing, New York, New York at 1-800-542-2595

Photo credits:

Images are courtesy of Shutterstock.com.
With thanks to Getty Images, Thinkstock Photo and iStockphoto.

Ian Struction – gjee. Grid – DistanceO. Front Cover – hudhud94, Nsit. 4 – Vasif Maharov, doyata. 5 – Andy Frith. 6–7 eveleen, Lucia Fox. 8 – NotionPic. 10 – diluck. 11 – Panda Vector, Webicon, PPVector. 12 – Svetlana Maslova, bsd. 13 – linear_design. 20–21 – Artco, Milta, Decobrush, rikkyall, justone, Chanut Wongrattana, PPVector. 22 – Bowrann. 23 – lastspark, AVIcon.

CONTENTS

Page 4	The Body Builders
Page 6	The Human Body
Page 8	The Human Lungs
Page 10	Parts of the Lungs
Page 12	Put It All Together
Page 14	Check It's Working
Page 16	Asthma
Page 18	Care for Your Lungs: Exercise
Page 20	Care for Your Lungs: Food
Page 22	Activities
Page 24	Glossary and Index

Words that look like <u>this</u> can be found in the glossary on page 24.

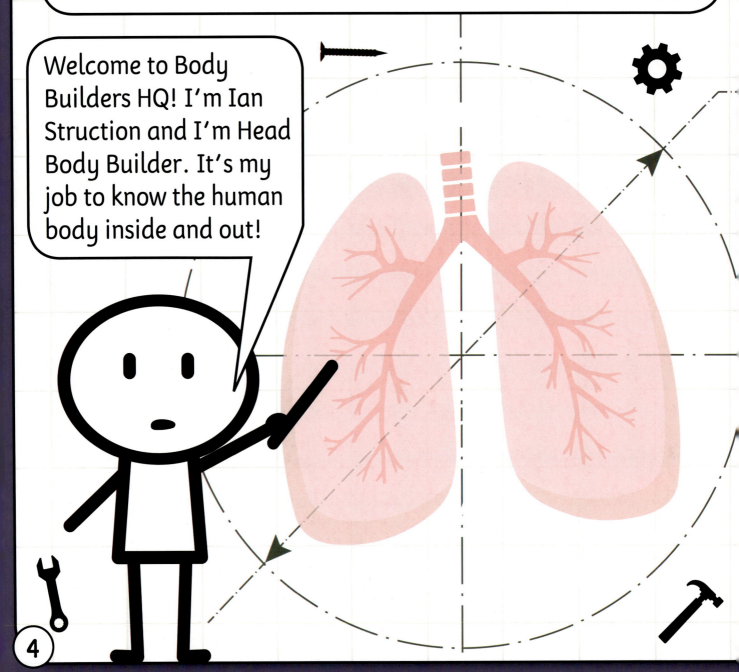

This instruction manual will teach you all about the human lungs. Look out for these signs to help you understand:

Do this

Don't do this

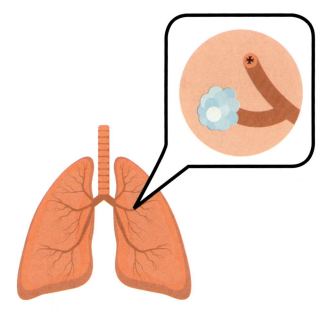

Zoom in on details

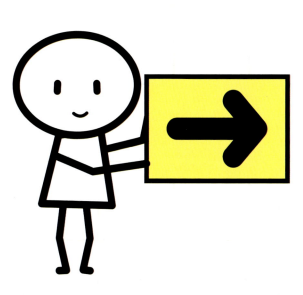

More information

THE HUMAN BODY

All the organs in the body have different jobs to do, and they all work together like a machine.

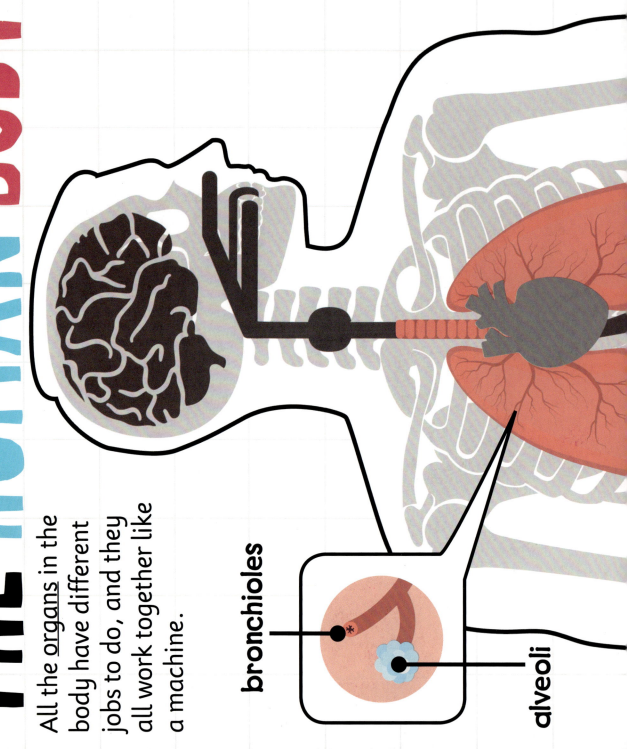

bronchioles

alveoli

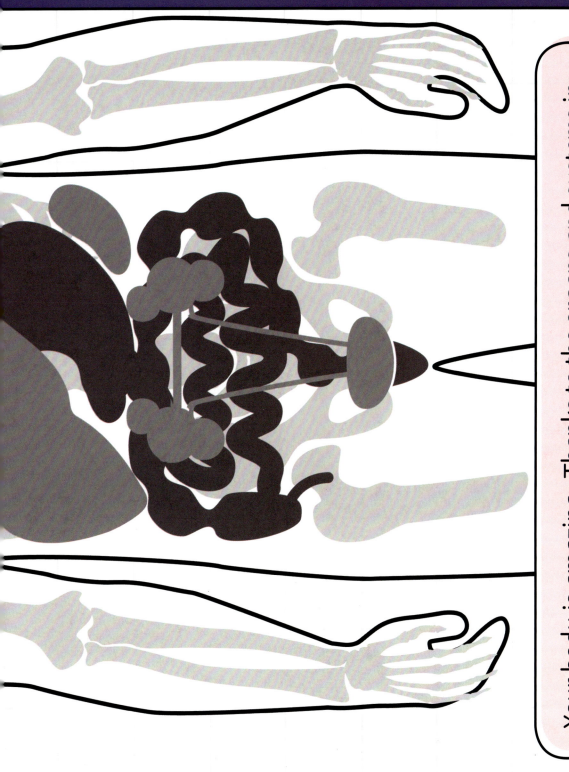

Your body is amazing. Thanks to the organs and systems in your body, you can do all sorts of things. You can breathe, think, eat, drink, and lots more!

THE HUMAN LUNGS

The lungs are air <u>sacs</u> found in the chest. When you breathe, air passes in and out of the lungs. The lungs take in <u>oxygen</u>, which we need to live.

- lungs come in pairs
- they take in oxygen
- one on each side of the chest
- breathe out <u>carbon dioxide</u>

→ You can live with only one lung.

8

You can feel and see your lungs working. Breathe in as far as you can, slow and steady, then breathe out. Your chest will rise and fall as you do this. Inside your chest, your lungs are filling with air and emptying again.

PARTS OF THE LUNGS

Let's look at the parts of the lungs.

right lung
Each lung is separated into sections, called lobes. The right lung has three lobes, and the left has two.

left lung
The left lung is slightly smaller than the right. This is because it has to make room for the heart.

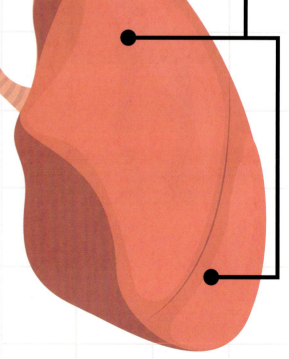

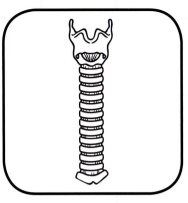

1x trachea
You breathe in through this tube.

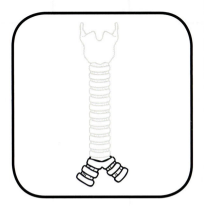

2 x bronchi
The trachea splits into two bronchi, like an upside-down Y in your chest.

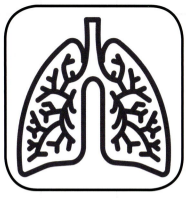

bronchioles
The bronchi split into lots of smaller tubes called bronchioles. Some are no thicker than a hair.

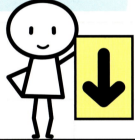

WHY IS THE DIAGRAM BACKWARDS?
"Left" and "right" on a diagram means the part that is on the person's left or right, not the page's. If you hold this book against you, facing outwards, the left and right will match yours.

alveoli
At the end of each bronchiole there is a <u>cluster</u> of small air sacs, like tiny balloons. This is where the blood picks up the oxygen from the air we breathe.

11

PUT IT ALL TOGETHER

The lungs work as part of the respiratory system. This means lots of body parts work together to help you breathe.

1x mouth and 1x nose
Air enters the body here.

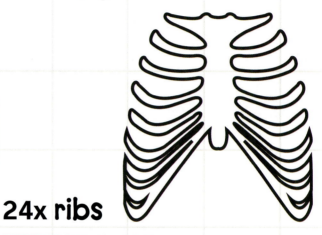

24x ribs
These bones form a cage, keeping your lungs and other organs safe. You have 12 pairs of ribs.

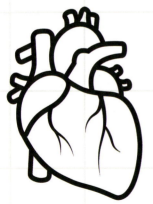

1x heart
This organ pumps blood to and from the lungs.

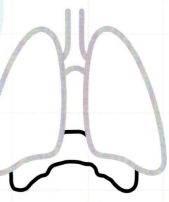

1x diaphragm
This large muscle at the bottom of the rib cage makes you breathe in and out.

Say "diaphragm" like this: DIE-uh-fram.

CHECK IT'S WORKING

The number of breaths you take in one minute is known as your breathing rate. You can test your breathing rate like this.

You will need:

1x stopwatch

1x partner

You will also need a chair and somewhere you can run around like a playground or your backyard. Start off sitting in the chair. Make sure you are not out of breath.

Breathe in and out normally, just the way you usually would. Ask your partner to count how many breaths you take in one minute. Record this in a table like this one:

| activity | breaths per minute ||
	Ian	Nurse
sitting in chair	18 breaths	16 breaths
standing up	20 breaths	19 breaths
after running around the playground or backyard	35 breaths	30 breaths

Now try filling in your table. Then swap and count your partner's breaths. What do you notice?

While sitting, a normal breathing rate for a child aged 5 to 12 is 12 to 25 breaths each minute.

ASTHMA

wheeeeeze wheeeeeze

Many people have asthma. People with asthma might make a wheezing sound when they breathe, or they might find it hard to breathe at times. Sometimes, their bronchioles squeeze themselves tight, and the breathing tubes get smaller.

Ways to Manage Asthma

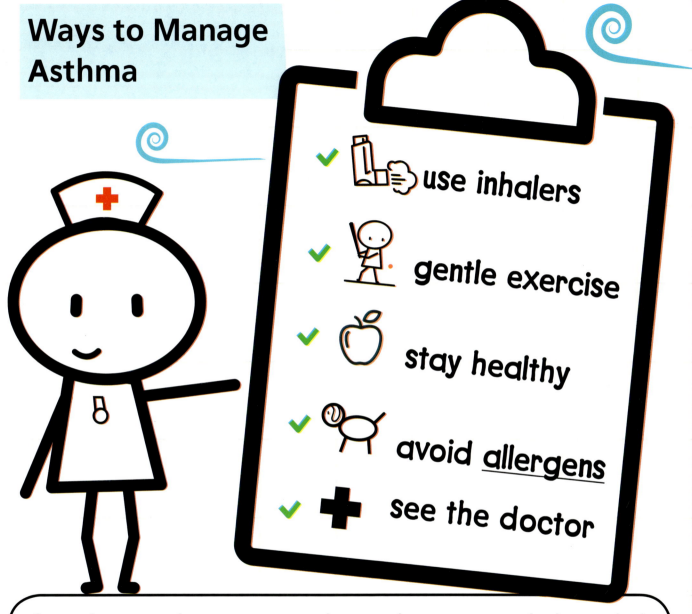

- use inhalers
- gentle exercise
- stay healthy
- avoid <u>allergens</u>
- see the doctor

If you have asthma, you might need to use an inhaler to help you breathe when it is difficult. It is especially important to take care of your lungs if you have asthma.

CARE FOR YOUR LUNGS: EXERCISE

By doing the right type of exercise, you can help your lungs work even better!

Why not try:

running

skipping rope

yoga

swimming

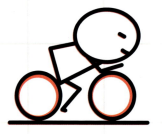
cycling

basketball

tennis

badminton

> You should aim for 60 minutes of activity each day, and at least three different activities each week. What's your favorite activity?

football

tag

skateboarding

Your breathing rate should get faster when you do these types of exercise. This is to get more oxygen to your muscles and other organs.

CARE FOR YOUR LUNGS: FOOD

To keep your lungs healthy, you need to breathe plenty of fresh, clean air. Did you know that what you eat can affect your lungs too?

pumpkins

papayas

spinach

yellow peppers

guavas

black beans

lentils

salmon

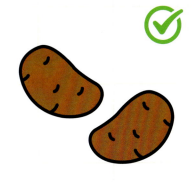
russet potatoes

apple juice

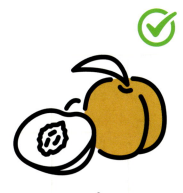
apricots

walnuts

blueberries

Eating a variety of foods helps keep your body healthy! This includes fruits, vegetables, and foods with fiber and healthy fats, like nuts.

21

ACTIVITIES

Breathing Rocks!

Can you rock the teddy to sleep just by breathing?

Sit on the floor with your favorite teddy resting against your tummy. Breathe in slowly and see your tummy and the teddy rise. Breathe out slowly and see teddy fall back.

A Happy Song

Singing can help your diaphragm and lungs grow stronger and can help you practice deep breathing. Maybe you can join your school choir—or even just sing in the shower!

GLOSSARY

allergens — things that are harmless for most people, but cause unwanted, bad reactions in others

carbon dioxide — a natural gas that is found in the air. Humans breathe it out.

cluster — a group of things, tightly packed together, that are alike

organs — parts of a living thing that have specific, important jobs to do to keep the body working properly

oxygen — a natural gas that living things need in order to survive

sacs — plant or animal parts that are shaped like a bag or pouch

systems — series of things that are connected and each have a job

waste — things left over that are no longer needed

INDEX

air 8–9, 11–13, 20
alveoli 6, 11, 13
asthma 16–17
breathing 7–9, 11–17, 19–20, 22–23

bronchi 11
bronchioles 6, 11, 16
chest 8–9, 11
diaphragm 12, 23

inhalers 17
lobes 10
oxygen 8, 11, 13, 19
singing 23